DISC

D0537054

9/07

DEMCO

Divorce

Divorce

Look for these and other books in the Lucent Overview Series:

Abortion
Acid Rain
Adoption
Advertising
Alcoholism
Animal Rights
Artificial Organs
The Beginning of Writing
The Brain
Cancer
Censorship
Chemical Dependency
Child Abuse
Children's Rights
Cities
The Collapse of the Soviet Union
Cults
Dealing with Death
Death Penalty
Democracy
Drug Abuse
Drugs and Sports
Drug Trafficking
Eating Disorders
Elections
Endangered Species
The End of Apartheid in South Africa
Energy Alternatives
Espionage
Ethnic Violence
Euthanasia
Extraterrestrial Life
Family Violence
Gangs
Garbage
Gay Rights
Genetic Engineering
The Greenhouse Effect
Gun Control
Hate Groups
Hazardous Waste

The Holocaust
Homeless Children
Homelessness
Illegal Immigration
Illiteracy
Immigration
Juvenile Crime
Memory
Mental Illness
Militias
Money
Ocean Pollution
Oil Spills
The Olympic Games
Organ Transplants
Ozone
The Palestinian-Israeli Accord
Pesticides
Police Brutality
Population
Poverty
Prisons
Rainforests
The Rebuilding of Bosnia
Recycling
The Reunification of Germany
Schools
Smoking
Space Exploration
Special Effects in the Movies
Sports in America
Suicide
The UFO Challenge
The United Nations
The U.S. Congress
The U.S. Presidency
Vanishing Wetlands
Vietnam
Women's Rights
World Hunger
Zoos

Divorce

by Liesa Abrams

LUCENT
BOOKS

THOMSON
★
GALE

San Diego • Detroit • New York • San Francisco • Cleveland • New Haven, Conn. • Waterville, Maine • London • Munich

THOMSON
✳
™
GALE

LIBRARY OF CONGRESS CATALOGING-IN-PUBLICATION DATA

Abrams, Liesa.
    Divorce / by Liesa Abrams.
        p. cm. — (Lucent overview series)
    Summary: Discusses the causes of divorce, its prevalence in the United States, and its
    effects on children, families, and society.
    Includes bibliographical references and index.
        ISBN 1-56006-197-9 (hardback : alk. paper)
        1. Divorce—United States—Juvenile literature. 2. Children of divorced parents—
    United States—Juvenile literature. [1. Divorce.] I. Title. II. Series.
        HQ834.A65 2004
        306.89—dc21
                                                                                2003009447

Printed in the United States of America

Contents

Introduction

Divorce—"As American as Apple Pie"

WHEN A BRIDE AND GROOM take their wedding vows, the couple pledge to be together "till death do us part." However, in close to half of all marriages in contemporary America this does not prove to be the case. Marriages end through divorce for many reasons. People change over time and may simply grow apart. Perhaps one or both members of a married couple fall in love with someone new. One spouse's career or personal goals might interfere with the relationship to the point of ending it. In extreme situations, verbal, physical, and/or sexual abuse leads one partner to end the marriage.

For the most part, the specific developments that might lead to divorce are difficult to predict when a couple get married. However, sociologists have identified several risk factors. Marriages begun before age twenty, second marriages, and marriages in which one or both spouses have divorced parents are all more likely to end in divorce. Couples with low income and education have higher rates of divorce than the rest of the population—although women with five or more years of college and good incomes are more likely to divorce than poor, less well-educated women. But no marriage is guaranteed safe from divorce, even when none of these risk factors are present.

Divorce's effects are far-reaching

Once a couple have made the decision to divorce, there are numerous issues to resolve. Many of them involve financial support, child custody, and how to ensure future happiness for all parties—especially the couple's children. In fact, divorce is far more complicated and problematic when the divorcing couple have children.

A couple with children cannot simply end their ties to each other and move on with their lives. The children will remain a common bond and common responsibility, potentially leading to more causes of dispute during and following the divorce process and raising an ongoing question of how to protect the children from the effects of the divorce. Psychologists, researchers, and lawmakers have therefore concentrated much of their attention to divorce on the children involved.

At the same time, sociologists point out that the effects of divorce can extend beyond children and reach society as a whole. If children of divorced parents become deeply troubled, society is affected in various ways. School performance tends to suffer, leading to a smaller likelihood that the child will pursue higher education. Greater incidences of juvenile delinquency, aggression, alcoholism, and drug abuse are all problems that will affect society at large.

Because of the many potential challenges divorce poses to children, families, and society, researchers have made great efforts to better understand why divorce happens and how to prevent it. They have given the issue special focus because, despite a prevailing belief among most Americans that divorce is something to be avoided, rates of divorce have historically been higher in the United States than in most other countries.

Almost half of all marriages in America end in divorce. Sociologists have identified several risk factors that contribute to divorce.

History of divorce in America

The roots of this contradiction can be traced all the way back to the first divorce in colonial America, awarded by Puritan leaders who defied English law and decided to grant divorce in certain cases. The Puritans did not approve of divorce itself; social attitudes condemned individuals who could not make their marriages work. However, the Puritans felt that allowing flawed marriages to end would strengthen the overall health of marriage and family in their community.

What the Puritans began, lawmakers continued as America became its own country. During and following the American Revolution, the national belief in America's right to a political "divorce" from England became tied to a similar sentiment in the arena of family life. "A philosophical preoccupation with the terms of union and disunion was central to republican thinking on both family and political relationships," writes author Barbara Dafoe Whitehead.[1] In fact, the first real jump in divorce rates in America occurred in the years after the Revolutionary War.

From that point forward, the divorce rate continued to climb steadily, particularly throughout the twentieth

century—even though divorce was still widely frowned upon. Various factors of American life and society were considered responsible. These included urbanization and industrialization, and the number of women entering the workforce because of the two world wars. The woman's rights movement was believed to play a major role, as was the increased standard of living for many Americans and the resulting shift in focus from financial security to emotional fulfillment. Women no longer necessarily needed marriage as a sole means of support, and men and women with access to more luxurious lifestyles had time to consider their general life satisfaction, since they no longer were consumed by a constant pressure to satisfy basic needs of survival.

Divorce in today's culture

As Americans watched the divorce rate skyrocket, sociologists and psychologists, disturbed and confused by the trend, continued to connect the situation to developments and conditions that were distinctly American. Many argued that underlying the various "causes" such as the woman's movement and the changing economy was the fundamentally American ideal of the individual's happiness taking priority over the needs of the group. This was the explanation for how a country that was generally less condoning of divorce than many others still had so many instances of divorce. In 1971, one American historian concluded that "divorce in the land of the free will continue to be as American as apple pie."[2]

Today, despite ongoing concern about negative consequences, it is predicted that 50 percent of all marriages in America will end in divorce. Given the prospect of divorce becoming the norm rather than the exception, most efforts focus on making the divorce process as fair and painless as possible, but this has proven challenging in itself. Disputes over support and custody are often complex, with no easy solutions at hand, and questions remain as to just how deeply adults, children, and society are affected by divorce—and how best to avoid the most dire consequences.

1

Child Custody— A Difficult Decision

WHEN A MARRIED couple reach the decision to divorce, the challenges of the process have only begun. For couples who have children, often the most important and wrenching challenge is deciding child custody. Many parents are able to reach a mutual agreement about custody outside of the courts, but in some cases the parents cannot agree and it is up to a judge to make the final declaration. Either way, the decision is a complicated one, requiring a great deal of thought. Over the years, families, lawyers, and lawmakers have struggled to find a way to resolve child custody questions as fairly as possible for everyone involved, but this has not been an easy task.

Legal custody—little controversy

When people use the word *custody*, they are most often referring to physical custody—the question of where and with which parent children will live after a divorce. But there are actually two different types of custody: physical and legal.

Legal custody means the authority to make major decisions for children, particularly involving education, medical issues, and religion. While in the past legal custody often went hand in hand with physical custody, that relationship has changed in recent decades. Today the majority of couples share legal custody even when one parent has sole physical custody of the children. Several states even require joint legal custody, except when this would clearly endanger the safety and well-being of the children or parent.

Sometimes parents fight for sole legal custody even when there is no threat of harm to anyone. For instance, a parent might wish to see his or her children pursue a religious path without the other parent's consent. However, as long as both parents can prove they are fit to be involved in these decisions, the courts try to award joint legal custody, forcing parents to work together even when they have different opinions on a major issue like religion.

Motivating this policy is the hope that if both parents legally remain both obligated and entitled to a degree of responsibility for their children, they will also remain involved in their children's lives, regardless of the physical custody arrangement. Studies so far have not shown much evidence that this is necessarily true, but parents are generally satisfied with sharing legal custody, and the decision rarely causes much controversy.

Child custody is the most difficult issue to face when couples divorce. The majority of couples decide to share legal custody even when one parent has physical custody.

Physical custody

On the other hand, physical custody can often lead to a good deal of conflict, both in and out of court. Before a divorce, both parents are accustomed to living with their children full-time. But this is no longer possible after divorce. No matter what decision about physical custody a couple come to—or are forced by a judge to agree to—there will be major changes in living

arrangements, and necessary compromises that do not always satisfy everyone.

There are numerous possible options for physical custody, and families continually make the effort to devise new and better arrangements. The most common resolution remains sole physical custody, overwhelmingly still given to mothers. According to one recent estimate, more than 85 percent of children live with their mothers after their parents divorce. However, more and more parents today are agreeing—or being forced by a judge to agree—to joint physical custody. Sometimes this means an exact split of the children's time between the two homes, but often the division is not perfectly equal. A child might go back and forth between mom's and dad's place every week or month, or might spend weekdays in one home and weekends in the other. Another possibility is that the split occurs between siblings, with one or more sibling living primarily with the mother and the other(s) living primarily with the father.

Physical custody of a child can be given to one parent or shared by both. In either case, the child usually spends time visiting and living with each parent.

Even when one parent is awarded sole physical custody, this does not mean that children will no longer see the other parent, referred to as the noncustodial parent. Usually a visitation schedule is set up so that the children visit with the noncustodial parent regularly. These visits might be during the day, or they might be overnight stays. They might take place once or even a few times a week, or they might be less frequent.

Clearly, custody arrangements are not simple, and there is a huge range of possible living situations for children whose parents divorce. While it is helpful to many families to have so many options to consider, sometimes parents—or judges, when the decision is in their hands—have difficulty choosing which is the best option for everyone involved.

Weighing alternatives

The truth is that no single custody arrangement always works best for every family or even for one family over lengthy time periods. In fact, even when efforts are made to find the ideal compromise for one particular family, every custody situation has its advantages and its disadvantages.

A common concern when parents divorce is that the relationship between the children and one or even both parents will suffer because of less time spent together. Therefore, many families try to ensure that children will remain involved with both parents by implementing different forms of joint custody, even if this causes problems of its own.

Lena experienced this difficulty firsthand when her parents divorced when she was ten years old. Lena's parents wanted to make sure not just that she saw enough of both of them, but also that the visits would be very frequent, with Lena never having to go more than a day without seeing one parent. So Lena's custody arrangement involved her going back and forth between her parents' homes every other day. Her parents lived only a few miles apart, so the travel itself was not difficult, and Lena was able to maintain strong ties with both parents. But Lena recalls feeling a great deal of stress and confusion over the constant upheaval. She was always worrying about remembering to bring what she needed from one home to the other. As she puts it, "I never knew where my underwear was!"[3]

Unfortunately, Lena's parents were still dealing with a lot of anger from the divorce, a common situation. So even though they set up a custody situation in which they would have regular contact with each other, neither parent was comfortable with the contact. Once, Lena's worst fear came true, and she did forget something she needed for a homework assignment at her father's home. Her mother refused to drive her back to pick up the item, unwilling to endure another face-to-face meeting with Lena's father.

In an effort to avoid this problem and provide children with more stability, many families decide that sole physical custody is a better solution. Children then have one home with all of their things, and they will not have to spend their time going back and forth between two homes. Even though sole physical custody is still the most common resolution, it carries its own drawbacks. Ellen lived with her mother after her parents divorced when she was a toddler. At first, Ellen visited her father regularly, staying with him every other weekend. But before long those visits became less and less frequent, eventually ending completely when Ellen's dad moved out of state.

"It was hard to stay close when he wasn't around for all of the little stuff in my life," Ellen says. "It was like both of our lives moved on, and we didn't have things to talk about anymore when I went to stay with him. He started to seem like a stranger, not my father, and I guess the more awkward I got around him, the less he felt like having me come stay with him. Then, by the time he moved away, it didn't even seem like that big a deal not to have him around."[4]

Ellen's point about the importance of "the little stuff" is echoed by many children and parents who face life after divorce. A nickname has even been coined—"Disneyland daddies"—for fathers who take their children for a weekend of ice cream and fun but miss out on the children's everyday needs, thoughts, and experiences, ingredients considered by many therapists as essential for true parent-child bonding.

Lena and Ellen can both point to bright sides of their custody arrangements—Lena's ongoing relationship with both parents and Ellen's sense of security regarding the home she lived in with her mother—and they can also easily identify the problems they faced. Their stories may be extreme examples, since joint custody is rarely sched-

uled on an every-other-day basis as it was for Lena, and many noncustodial parents do continue to stay involved in their children's lives, unlike Ellen's father. However, most children whose parents divorce have a similar feeling that their custody arrangements are compromises that fail to provide complete satisfaction.

How is the decision made?

Since each custody arrangement has its own benefits and flaws, it is far from easy for families and courts to decide what the best strategy is for a particular situation. Many factors are considered in making the decision, each carrying more or less weight, depending on the circumstances.

When parents cannot agree on custody and the case is brought to a judge to decide, judges commonly take into account several factors. They consider where and with which parent the child is living at the time of divorce (if parents are already living separately), the age and gender of the child, and each parent's ability to provide a secure, stable home. If one parent works many hours and would rarely be home when the child is, the judge might consider awarding sole custody to the other parent. In recent years, courts have sometimes awarded mothers custody of daughters and fathers of sons, after research suggested the importance of children living with a same-sex role model. However, there are few absolute rules determining a custody decision. The primary exception involves cases where abuse is involved. If one parent has proved to be a potential threat to the safety of the other parent or the children, that parent's access to the children will be limited if not prevented altogether.

These primary factors that help judges decide custody cases today—age, gender, and the strength of the existing relationships between children and their parents—all revolve around one basic concept. This concept, called the "best interests of the child," has its roots in a law from early in the twentieth century.

"Tender years"

Originally American wives and children were considered the property of husbands and fathers. So when a divorce was granted, which was far rarer than it is today, the fathers would nearly always receive custody of their children. This changed in the early 1900s, when there was an increasing cultural focus on the importance of a mother's nurturing love. Much attention was given to the work of Sigmund Freud, the first prominent expert in the field of psychoanalysis. Freud's writings on the bond between mothers and young children fueled a growing belief that this bond should be respected above all else. This belief was reflected in new laws stating that children of "tender years" should not be separated from their mothers in the event of a divorce.

At first, tender years was defined as ending at age seven, but the notion broadened over time to mean that children of any age were better off with their mothers. The tender years assumption was not intended as a switch from favoring fathers to favoring mothers. Instead it was meant to change the emphasis from the needs and rights of either parent to those of the children. Eventually the term *tender years* was replaced by the phrase "the best interests of the child," to clarify this as the central issue in deciding custody. But until the 1970s, it was generally accepted that it was in the best interests of children to live with their mothers, and there were very few cases of sole custody awarded to fathers or even joint physical custody.

Sigmund Freud's theories about the special bond between mother and child fueled the belief that children should be placed with their mothers in divorce cases.

Women's rights and fathers' rights

The concept that children would fare best if raised by their mothers was challenged when society's views of gender roles began to change in the 1960s and 1970s. Women had been entering the workforce in increasing numbers since the 1940s, and now a movement for women's rights argued that women were capable of taking on any job a man could do and should be treated equally to men in every respect. Women arguing this point eventually joined together to form an organization, the National Organization for Women (NOW), to support their cause. "We reject . . . that home and family are primarily woman's world and responsibility—hers, to dominate—

his to support," NOW declared in its founding statement in 1967. "We believe that a true partnership between the sexes demands a different concept of marriage, an equitable sharing of the responsibilities of home and children."[5] This meant there was no reason to assume a woman's role was in the home rather than in an office. But making this claim led to a question of whether women possessed unique nurturing abilities necessary for raising children.

Meanwhile, fathers who believed they were as qualified as their ex-wives to nurture their children began to organize their own movement. They essentially made the same point, that men and women should be on equal footing on the issue of child custody. If women were no longer bound by strict gender roles, these men argued, then there was no reason for men to be either.

Equalizing the playing field

Just as women's rights proponents achieved some success in changing social attitudes and laws to support their cause, fathers' rights advocates began to see a response to the strong challenge they mounted to the preference for mothers in custody cases. The changing tide of thought was evidenced in the public reaction to the 1979 hit movie *Kramer vs. Kramer.* The film featured actor Dustin Hoffman as a father fighting for custody of his son. Moviegoers flocked to see the film, and most sympathized with the plight of Hoffman's character, as public sentiment began to turn toward supporting the struggle of real-life fathers facing the same battle Hoffman faced on-screen.

Psychologists and social scientists, meanwhile, went to work to determine if in fact men were equally suited to being the primary custodial parents. Their findings, for the most part, supported the idea. Early studies found that children whose fathers were more involved in their lives performed better academically. These children also showed greater ability to get along with peers and had higher levels of self-esteem, among other positive qualities. On the other hand, children whose fathers were less involved were more likely to become juvenile delinquents.

Experts agreed that fathers were as important to healthy children as mothers were, but the question remained whether children who lived with their fathers rather than their mothers would lose out on some larger, more essential benefit. Most research showed they would not. Author Richard A. Warshak, one of the leading experts in this area of research, concluded that "the psychological status of children living with their fathers was comparable to children of the same ages living with their mothers. Father-custody children, on the average, do not look any better than mother-custody children and they do not look any worse."[6]

With psychology supporting the cause of fathers' rights and elements of popular culture such as *Kramer vs. Kramer* reflecting a similar belief in the American public, the legal system began to react. One by one, courts across the country abolished laws that explicitly favored mothers in custody cases. By 1982, just seven states officially gave preference to mothers for children of tender years.

But changing a law on paper does not always change how cases are decided—it is hard to measure how subtle prejudices might still influence a judge's decision. The truth is that mothers are still more likely than fathers to receive custody when the parents bring their custody battle to court. One study found that mothers were granted the form of custody they requested roughly twice as often as fathers were.

Fathers blame this situation on a lingering "motherhood mystique," a belief they say many people still hold that mothers remain ultimately suited for nurturing. Some mothers, however, argue that this motherhood mystique can work against them as well. They make the point that if they fail to live up to the expected standard for the role of a mother, they may lose custody of their children. The case of Jennifer Ireland made headlines in 1994. Ireland lost custody of her daughter, Maranda, to the child's father

Jennifer Ireland (left) made headlines in 1994 when custody of her daughter was awarded to the child's father. Ireland appealed and was awarded custody in 1995.

because Ireland had been sending Maranda to day-care while Ireland attended college classes. The father himself worked, but his mother was available to watch Maranda. The judge presiding over Maranda's custody case decided that Maranda would be better off with a father who had a blood relative to babysit than with a mother who considered day-care sufficient.

Many working mothers have faced a similar struggle when fighting for custody. Often these women feel they are unfairly penalized for needing to support themselves and their children. Author Dawn Bradley Berry found evidence to support this claim. She refers to a study conducted in Massachusetts that found that "women who temporarily separated from their children for any reason risked losing custody, whereas men who were absent for years without paying child support could return and gain custody."[7]

Gender politics?

Fathers continue to fight for a system that views them as equal to mothers, while mothers work just as hard to keep from becoming victims of gender stereotypes themselves. Some experts, however, point out that the emphasis has shifted to being fair to the adults involved, instead of serving the best interests of the children. Author Mary Ann Mason writes: "As a society, we no longer agree on what is good for children. We are more

focused instead on the political rights of parents. . . . I have witnessed the laws governing custody disputes swing wildly over the past two (nearly three) decades. None of these radical swings in the law was prompted by new research findings about what is good for children. Each emerged from a skirmish in the larger arena of gender politics."[8]

According to children's rights advocates, it is dangerous to base child custody laws on societal attitudes toward the true roles of women or the rights of fathers because this approach carries a risk of ignoring what is best for the children involved. The bottom line, the advocates say, should not be fairness to mothers or fathers, but fairness to children.

Even among children's rights advocates, however, there is dissent over the issue of custody. Some argue that joint custody—equal access to both parents—is an essential right for children. Others believe that children will fare best living primarily with one parent—whichever parent was most involved in the child's daily life before the divorce. Neither side of the debate has been able to prove definitively that its solution is best for children, and there is still no clear answer as to what custody arrangement does fulfill this aim.

No easy answer

With this uncertainty in mind, many experts continue to search for innovative solutions to the dilemma of custody. In several recent cases, the children have retained "custody" of the family home; the parents are the ones who take turns moving in and out so that they can share joint physical custody without the children having to experience too much disruption in their daily lives. Of course, this is rarely a practical option for various financial and logistical reasons, and it could easily prove to have its own drawbacks as well.

One point that researchers emphasize is that custody arrangements can and should be flexible. What works best for a family might change over time, so appropriate adaptations to original agreements should always be possible. Courts have made efforts to incorporate this notion into their decisions, and families who settle custody without a legal dispute have likewise tried to remain open-minded as time passes.

The question of child custody remains a source of much heated debate, and the search for ultimate fairness a true challenge. Unfortunately, at this time there is still no perfect solution for anyone involved.

2

Financial Support

EVEN AFTER CHILD custody has been decided, the divorce process still poses further challenges. At the top of the list are the issues of spousal and child support—whether either or both are to be awarded and, if so, in what amounts. Often the attempts to resolve these questions can become as contentious as the debate over child custody. And in the case of child support, the discussion can become intertwined with that of custody. Spousal support, however, is viewed separately from both child support and child custody, although that does not prevent it from causing its own share of controversy.

Spousal support—yesterday's alimony

Originally, spousal support was called alimony and served a different function than it does today. The traditional nuclear family upheld as a model in the 1950s was made up of a husband who worked outside the home and a wife whose responsibilities in the marriage revolved around the home and child-rearing. When a couple divorced, the wife was awarded alimony because she was not expected to be able to support herself. Usually these payments ended if a woman remarried, because she would presumably be supported by her new husband thereafter.

Over time, several factors changed the policy of alimony. First, with the woman's movement, more women were entering the workforce. It was no longer true that wives would almost always leave a marriage without the means to support themselves. Although women were still earning less than men, it was difficult to continue to argue for alimony while at the same time demanding equality across the board. "The expectation is that women [now] are ready, willing, and able to support themselves," explains author Esther M. Berger.[9]

At the same time, a major change in divorce law occurred. Until 1970, every divorce was ruled to be the fault of one of the parties. To win alimony, a woman typically would prove that the divorce was her husband's fault. But the creation of no-fault divorce allowed a couple to sue for divorce on the basis of mutually agreed-upon terms, without assigning blame to either spouse. So when a husband was no longer perceived by the law as responsible for the divorce, and a wife was able and likely to earn her own income following the divorce, alimony was not deemed necessary.

What is spousal support in today's world?

Today what was once called alimony is known as spousal support. Although it is not awarded as commonly as alimony once was, spousal support is still an issue that frequently comes up during a divorce, and with an economy and society that grow more complex all the time, it is a difficult issue to resolve.

With the change in gender roles, women are no longer presumed to need—or deserve—spousal support. However, in certain cases support is still awarded. The difference is that payments tend to be smaller than in the past, and they are usually granted only for a limited time period rather than stretching indefinitely into the future. The payments are viewed as a temporary adjustment to assist the spouse in recovering from the divorce and learning necessary job skills, with the idea that nothing will prevent the spouse from eventually finding work.

Another change from the past is that the spouse who is awarded support is not necessarily the woman. Men are equally entitled to sue for spousal support, because in today's world a husband may earn less income than his wife or even no income at all.

How determinations are made

When divorcing couples are unable to make decisions about their financial future alone, the issue is brought to court as part of the divorce case. A judge then faces the difficult task of ruling on spousal support.

The primary factors that affect whether spousal support will be granted are the incomes of both spouses, the work history of the spouses prior to separation, and the duration of the marriage. When there is a large gap between incomes and one spouse (still more often the wife) relied heavily upon the other spouse's means of support during

Pictured is a family of the 1950s relaxing in their living room. Throughout the 1950s, divorced women were awarded alimony because it was thought they were unable to support themselves.

Couples unable to agree on spousal support rely on a judge to make the determination. The judge considers the income and work history of the spouses and the duration of their marriage.

the marriage, spousal support is likely to be awarded. This is particularly the case if the marriage lasted a significant number of years; in one study by Eleanor E. Macoby and Robert H. Mnookin, couples who were granted spousal support had been married at least twelve years on average.

After these common and significant factors are considered, judges might have to look at additional factors. Sometimes a spouse will argue that he or she played an instrumental role during the marriage in helping the other spouse build a career or business that will bring in a great deal of money in the years after the divorce. When there is evidence supporting this claim, the spouse might be awarded spousal support as a form of repayment for his or her contribution to the earnings. The matter can become even more complicated when divorcing couples also consider other future income, such as social security payments and retirement pensions.

Once a judge decides that spousal support is called for in a specific situation, the next issue is how much the payments should be and how long they should last. Again, the two respective incomes are considered in answering these questions, as is the earning potential of the spouse being awarded support. Berger offers an example of a wife who has a law degree but has not practiced law for several years. Even though her husband was supporting her during those years, she has the training to earn a substantial income herself after the divorce.

The duration of the marriage will also affect the amount of support awarded. Macoby and Mnookin's study found, for example, that spousal support awards increased slightly for each additional year of marriage.

When conflict arises

Although length of marriage is an indisputable fact, the other factors that come into play in determining spousal support awards can be somewhat murky. In deciding support amounts, a judge has to weigh carefully the capacity of one spouse to make payments and the capacity of the other spouse to earn a reliable and sufficient income. In addition, further complications and controversies often arise during the process of determining spousal support.

It certainly seems fair that if women are able to make their own living, their ex-husbands should be under no obligation to continue to support them. However, there is often a difference between a theoretical ability to hold a job and actually being able to support oneself. "Although the court may see a strong, intelligent forty-year-old woman who appears capable of doing many types of work, the same woman may in fact have been a homemaker and mother since she was twenty and is therefore entering the workforce in the same position as a much younger, inexperienced worker," argues lawyer Dawn Bradley Berry.[10] On the surface, there is no reason this woman should not be able to find and keep a job. But the reality of discrimination against older women who have been out of the workforce could be a real obstacle to her, and she might also find it difficult to adjust to a new way of life after years of being a homemaker and mother.

Taking this scenario a step further, if a mother is awarded primary physical custody of her children, she might face difficulty balancing a job that brings in enough income to support her household with her responsibilities as caretaker for the children. A common complaint is that a large portion of the income earned must go to another source of child care once the mother is no longer at home with her children.

On the other hand, spouses (typically husbands) who are ordered by a judge to pay large amounts of spousal support based upon their income may also feel that the decision is unfair. Men worry that they will be unable to support a new wife and family if they are obligated to give a large portion of their income to their ex-wives. Also, some men have complained that they no longer have the freedom to make choices about their jobs, which could mean a decrease in income. Or they feel that they are being taken advantage of and that their former spouses could make more of an effort to find work. These men view spousal support as an outdated notion that no longer makes sense in today's society.

Men are not the only ones who feel that their ex-spouses take advantage of them with spousal support. Lana, whose husband asked for a divorce after close to thirty years of marriage, says that she was so deeply in shock at the time that she did not challenge anything her husband offered or even study their final agreement very closely. When he then married the woman he had had an affair with in the very early years of his marriage to Lana, she became further lost in her profound emotional trauma. Lana was left with three children, two in college and one still in high school. Initially, her ex-husband sent regular spousal support payments that were enough to supplement Lana's moderate income. Once her youngest child was in college, however, the payments were cut in half, forcing Lana to move to a smaller home, even though her daughter still lived with her. Lana says she had a great deal of trouble confronting her ex-husband when she was still grappling with her anger; having to see him or interact

with him at all was so painful that she did what she could to avoid it.

Because the issue of spousal support has proven so problematic, judges are usually careful to make flexible rulings that can change along with circumstances in the parties' lives. For instance, if a spouse charged with paying support suffers a drop in income beyond his or her control, this will be taken into account. Likewise, if the spouse receiving support begins to earn a significant income, this could warrant a second look at the support agreement.

Currently this policy of keeping spousal support malleable and ascertaining when it is truly needed is viewed as the best possible solution to a difficult issue. But many people still contend that resolutions are often unfair to one or both spouses.

When couples divorce, women with physical custody of the children often worry about balancing a job and caring for the children.

Child support

Child support—payments allotted specifically for the children's needs—is decided separately from spousal support, and its sole purpose is to provide for the divorcing couple's children. Unlike in the case of spousal support, there is no need to prove that children require financial support after their parents' divorce. Instead, the debate concerns how much responsibility each parent will carry for this support.

Again, the answer to this question is not always clearcut. Since the majority of custody arrangements still leave one parent with sole physical custody, child support payments are typically awarded to the custodial parent, to be paid by the noncustodial parent. Custodial parents who have substantially higher incomes than noncustodial parents may not receive child support payments, however. Also, in certain cases of joint physical custody, one parent

One of the many variables in the cost of raising children is their extracurricular activities. Participation in sports like baseball involves additional expenses.

might still pay the other parent child support. This could occur, for example, if even part-time child care is too high a drain on the significantly lower income of one spouse.

With so many variables to consider, judges often face difficult choices. In an effort to make the process simpler, Congress passed the Family Support Act in 1988. While other aspects of divorce law vary from state to state, the act established national guidelines for ensuring the security of children of divorce. These guidelines estimated the expense of raising children and also set national standards for judges to consider in determining child support awards. These factors include the number of children, the income earned by each parent, and the amount of time that the children will spend with each parent. The guidelines are not mandatory, and courts still have the freedom to adapt their rulings to the unique circumstances of every family. But the factors highlighted in the Family Support Act are most often what determines a final decree.

In particular, the income of the parents is usually the most significant factor. One study found that most noncustodial fathers were ordered to pay child support, although most custodial fathers did not receive child support from the noncustodial mothers. This was explained by the average difference in incomes between the mothers and fathers, with the fathers earning more than twice what the mothers earned.

Sources of dispute

The issue of child support appears straightforward upon first glance. Everyone agrees that children need to be supported, and making the decision based on who can afford the support and who will be doing the caretaking seems to make sense.

Unfortunately, it is often not this simple. The first problem many couples face is that it is difficult to accurately determine the costs of raising a child. Basic expenses such as food, clothing, and shelter are obvious, but there are also extras such as sports equipment, spending money, or a car. Sometimes a custodial parent will argue that the amount of support he or she receives is not sufficient to provide the children with the things they deserve or that the amount of support decided upon when the child was young needs to change as the child grows.

Particularly, there has been much debate over whether child support payments should terminate when children reach legal adulthood at age eighteen or whether parents should be under obligation to contribute toward a college education. Even parents who remain married are not required to provide financial support to their grown children. However, divorcing spouses and their college-bound children often argue that had the marriage lasted, the spouse with the income to afford college would have paid for it, and the divorce should not change this—as it usually does.

Spouses charged with paying child support feel there are injustices on their side as well. Some parents making the payments object to having no say in how the money is spent. Other parents making child support payments claim that their ex-spouses are using the money on themselves, not their children. "I agreed to pay extra at the time of the divorce so the girls could have a private parochial education," says divorced father Tom Murphy. "I later found out that [my ex-wife] was using the tuition money for other things . . . like summer cottages and vacations with her boyfriend. I had to buy [my daughters] essentials like gym shoes and glasses on my own, in addition to paying child support, if I wanted to be sure they got the things they needed."[11]

The problematic connection between physical custody and child support

Even when the question of where child support payments are going is not a source of tension, numerous other conflicts are possible. One of the most controversial aspects of child support decisions is the way in which they are linked to child custody. According to the 1988 Family Support Act, a family's physical custody arrangement is an important factor for judges to consider when deciding responsibility and amount of child support payments. This is a reasonable consideration, since the parent who must house, feed, and take care of the children needs resources with which to do so.

Beyond this basic connection, courts in some states have directly linked child support payments to the exact amount of time a child spends in each parent's home. In California, for example, the more frequently that children visit a noncustodial parent, the less he or she will have to pay in child support. The logic behind this idea is twofold: First, the custodial parent does not need as much support if the other parent has an increased responsibility for the children; second, there is the hope that an incentive of smaller child support awards would encourage noncustodial parents to remain involved in their children's lives.

However, many researchers point out certain problems accompanying a connection between child custody and child support—problems that are difficult to avoid. One danger is that a parent could use the issue of custody to bargain for smaller support payments. "Fathers who may have no real desire for custody threaten mothers with the possible loss of custody . . . in order to win concessions in property division and family support," warns child custody expert Mary Ann Mason.[12] In other words, a father might sue for partial or full custody to reduce the amount of child support he will be asked to pay. A mother desperate for custody then might pull back on the amount of support she is requesting so that the father will withdraw his plea for custody. One California divorce attorney acknowledges this tactic, saying "about sixty percent of my male clients ask for joint custody now, but only ten percent really want it. It's a good bargaining position."[13]

While this concern is generally recognized as valid, some researchers have found that this situation does not occur as frequently as this lawyer claims. In another study, fathers for the most part did not seem to be strategically bargaining for lower support payments, and even if some were, mothers were not forced to give up ground on custody to win more support.

The problem can extend beyond courtroom negotiations, however. Even well-meaning fathers who file for joint custody (or request a significant amount of visitation) out of a genuine desire to parent their children can find themselves unable to fulfill expectations after the divorce. On paper, the father plans and expects to spend enough time taking care of the children so that his child support payments to his ex-wife are reduced accordingly. However, in reality the children end up spending more time with the mother than originally imagined. Meanwhile, the mother has experienced a large drop in income after the divorce and finds that the reduced support payments are not sufficient to provide for the children.

Michelle, a divorced mother, experienced this problem firsthand. She agreed to a proposed fifty-fifty joint custody arrangement with her ex-husband, John, meaning that even though his salary was triple hers, she would receive very little child support. Once the custody arrangement was under way, however, John had trouble actually keeping the children with him for the proposed amount of time. "From the beginning John asked to change his days because of work," Michelle said. "His time got less and less. Now (almost two years later) the kids spend only two or three nights a month at his place at most. I'm happy I don't have to send them away—I just need my fair share of child support."[14]

When the check does not come

Simply awarding one party in a divorce specified child support, even when the amount is considered fair by everyone involved, does not guarantee the money will be paid. The issue of enforcing child support payments remains one of the most difficult challenges in the divorce process. Many women report a drop-off in payments as time passes; checks are sent late or for less money than required. Sometimes payments cease completely.

There are many possible reasons for this. Noncustodial parents sometimes withhold support for strategic reasons to influence the other parent's decisions about the children.

For instance, if a noncustodial father does not believe his son should drive, he might not send the child support payment that he knows will go toward car insurance. Other times the noncustodial parent will refuse to pay child support until the custodial parent agrees to a visitation schedule that the noncustodial parent prefers.

Some fathers, meanwhile, claim that they are unable to make the payments for reasons out of their control and that the law does not allow for this. One divorced father said, "When I was unemployed for several months after the company I worked for went bankrupt, there was no adjustment in my child support obligation."[15] Some noncustodial parents are also resentful of support decisions they feel are unfair. This father also noted that although his own remarriage led a judge to raise the amount of his child support payments—because his combined household income had grown—his wife's remarriage was not taken into consideration. Resentment, some experts contend, may also contribute to the dilemma of noncompliance.

Some fathers sue for custody as a means of reducing child support payments. Others sincerely want custody, but are unable to meet the emotional needs of the children.

In response, county and state governments have developed a range of services to enforce child support payments when parents cannot solve the problem themselves. Government offices, for example, can order a man to undergo DNA testing to establish paternity and responsibility for child support. Local agencies can issue child support orders and withhold money from paychecks to enforce them. Child support service agencies are also trained in locating noncustodial parents and advising custodial parents about bringing a civil suit or even criminal charges to collect back payments. Despite such efforts, however, nationwide average figures show that 50 percent of children receive their court-ordered support, 25 percent receive partial payments, and 25 percent receive no payment.

Many problems, few solutions

Although spousal and child support appear to be clear-cut issues, a closer look reveals that they hold the potential to cause a great deal of conflict and controversy. Difficult questions remain as to how to resolve disputes in as fair a manner as possible for everyone involved. As with child custody, there are no easy answers. But experts realize how crucial it is to continue to search for these answers in the hopes of reducing the devastating effect divorce can have on parents and children.

3

Consequences of Divorce for Children

WHEN PARENTS DIVORCE, their children are clearly affected in numerous ways. The most obvious changes involve new living arrangements and possibly new relationships with one or both parents. While no one would argue that divorce is a painless experience for children, there has been a great deal of debate over the years about just how deep and long-lasting the painful effects of parental divorce are on children.

To answer this question and fully examine the issue of divorce's impact on children, experts first attempt to distinguish between short- and long-term effects. Short-term effects encompass children's direct reactions to their parents' divorce during the event and in the following two years. Psychologists identity long-term effects as problems that continue for more than two years or that develop for the first time several years after the divorce—including when the children have become adults.

Adjustment disorders

In the short term, there is little disagreement that children whose parents are going through a divorce commonly experience various problems adjusting to the disruption in their lives. Psychologists who have studied children of divorce over the years have identified certain patterns of symptoms called "adjustment disorders" in children who are experiencing difficulty getting used to the changes in their lives. Adjustment disorders are defined by different behaviors at different ages.

Preschool children whose parents divorce typically become very emotional, with frequent angry or sad outbursts and incidents such as nightmares or bed-wetting. Often they fear being apart from one or both parents and also start to act younger than their ages, going back to behaviors they had seemed to outgrow. "For example," explains psychologist and author Edward Teyber, "children may resume sucking their thumbs, carrying a security blanket, asking for a pacifier, hitting their siblings, or needing help to feed themselves."[16]

Children between six and eight are prone to sadness and a feeling that they have been rejected by the parent who "left" the marriage and home. They are likely to cry frequently. School performance typically drops among children in this age group because they have difficulty concentrating on anything other than their sadness.

Anger is the primary emotional response in children aged nine to twelve, and it is often expressed through aggressive behavior. Many of these children have trouble getting along with peers and develop problems responding to discipline, both at home and in school. "Many single-parent mothers report that it is impossible to discipline their nine- to twelve-year-old sons," Teyber writes.[17] This is also the age group in which physical complaints such as headache or stomachache are most common.

Adolescents are already beginning the process of separation from their parents as they approach adulthood, so they do not always exhibit the extreme symptoms of adjustment disorders seen in younger children. The typical response for teenagers is to continue to withdraw from their parents, often to a more significant degree than teenagers in intact families. Some actually show positive reactions, becoming more mature and helping their parent or parents in the care of younger siblings.

Other teenagers, however, slide toward unhealthy behaviors such as drug use or promiscuity. Statistics have shown that children of divorce are prone to these problems—they are more likely to be juvenile delinquents, to drop out of school, and to get pregnant as teenagers. Several studies have even linked divorce to higher rates of teen suicide and homicide.

Girls versus boys

Within these age groups, there are also differences based on gender. Many of the adjustment disorder symptoms have been found to occur more frequently in boys than in girls.

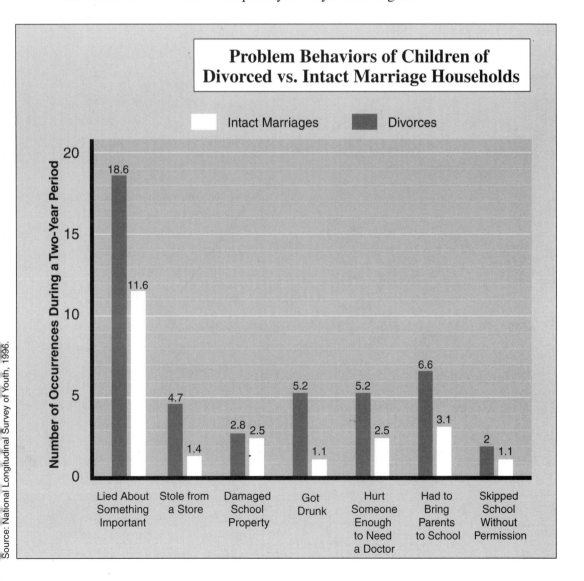

Problem Behaviors of Children of Divorced vs. Intact Marriage Households

Source: National Longitudinal Survey of Youth, 1996.

Young boys tend to become more needy and immature than young girls, and older boys more aggressive and difficult to discipline. This phenomenon is particularly evident in boys living with their mothers, which is the most common custody arrangement. "After Robert and I divorced, my son Josh, who had always been very amicable, suddenly became unruly," says Beth. "He began throwing tantrums all the time, especially after returning from a visit with his father. He would tell me that he didn't have to listen to me, because Dad didn't make him do any chores at his apartment."[18]

Young boys typically have a harder time adjusting to divorce than young girls. Boys often become extremely needy and difficult to discipline.

Young girls seem to adapt more easily to divorce. They generally show fewer symptoms than boys and experience these symptoms for a shorter period of time. However, adolescent girls whose fathers withdraw significantly from their lives following the divorce sometimes suffer from very low self-esteem. They also tend to become sexually active sooner and with more partners than adolescent girls in intact families.

Parental conflict the real problem?

Many experts acknowledge that these problems are real and pervasive but argue that divorce itself is not the root cause of adjustment disorders and delinquency in children. Instead, they say that the fighting between parents is the real problem. Tension between the parents usually builds in the time leading up to the decision to divorce and often continues after the divorce. Teyber says, "Children are more likely to develop personality and behavior problems in unhappy, unloving families in which the parents fight continually than in any other kind of family situation. . . . The degree of marital discord is one of the most important determinants of children's adjustment in every type of family."[19]

Many studies support this view. Some even go a step further, arguing that children are actually better off after a divorce because they are living in households with less daily tension. The National Institute of Mental Health surveyed more than a thousand children to investigate this idea. The study found that children living with a divorced parent had fewer behavioral problems than children living with married parents who fought constantly. Likewise, a study released in 2002 by Ohio State University sociology professor Yongmin Sun and statistician Yuanzhang Li showed the potential for divorce to ease children's stress. Children in the study had an increasing number of problems in the time leading up to their parents' divorce, suffered the worst symptoms right at the time of divorce, and then gradually returned to healthier states in the several years following.

Amy's experiences support this idea. Amy's parents divorced when she was fifteen, after years of terrible fighting, and the two years following the divorce were far easier for her than the years leading up to it. "I've always said that [my parents'] divorce was the best thing they did for each other, and I still think that's true," says Amy, now twenty-seven. "My dad didn't stop badmouthing my mom [after the divorce], and that bothered me, but my mom became very gracious about my dad. She encouraged my brother and I to have fun while we were with him and enjoy our time together; it was as though she was able to see him in a different light when he wasn't making her daily life miserable. I was relieved. There was so much less fighting in our house, so much less tension. And I was finally able to get along with my dad in a way I never had before."[20]

Deep scars

Divorce, however, does not always provide an end to marital conflict. According to one study, a third of the divorced couples in the study group were fighting with as much bitterness and anger ten years after their divorces were final as they had been at the time of their divorce. For various reasons, many parents continue to have a high level of conflict after divorcing. This is one possible explanation for the severe adjustment disorders that persist in many children of divorce.

There are two major schools of thought on the subject of the long-term impact of divorce on children. Some researchers claim that divorce presents serious obstacles to the ability of these children to later lead healthy and satisfying adult lives. The other school suggests instead that after two years, the majority of children are well on the road to recovery. During the early decades of research into the question, most experts aligned themselves with one camp or the other.

One of the first researchers to take an in-depth look at this topic was Judith Wallerstein, who found that children of divorce suffered deep and long-lasting scars. In 1971, Wallerstein and her associates began a study in which she interviewed sixty families from Marin County, California, who were going through a divorce. A total of 131 children and adolescents were involved in the study, which was intended to be completed after one year. However, follow-up interviews that took place between a year and eighteen months after each divorce convinced Wallerstein that the children and their parents were still enduring a great deal of turmoil. A five-year interview was planned and then another round of interviews at the ten-year mark. When Wallerstein found that children were still suffering from the divorce, she added a fifteen-year check-in and then finally a landmark twenty-five-year follow-up.

Wallerstein's results all support the concern that the impact of divorce on children is long-lasting and profound. For example, Wallerstein compares the childhood memories shared by children of intact families with the memo-

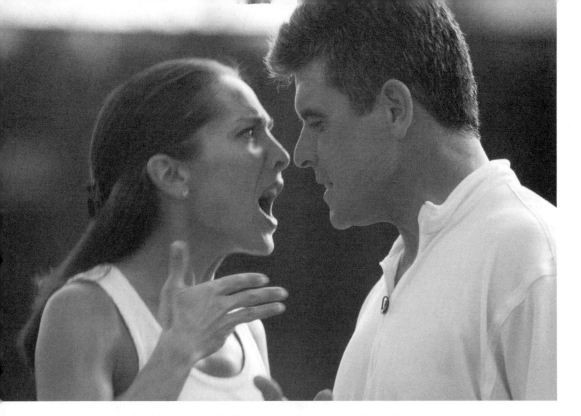

ries shared by children of divorce. After describing how Gary, whose parents stayed married, remembers playing in the tree house in his backyard, Wallerstein notes that children of divorce do not talk about these kinds of "play" memories when questioned about their lives. "No doubt many [children of divorced parents] rode bicycles, climbed trees, and fooled around in backyards," Wallerstein writes, "but *they did not mention it.* . . . Instead of caring about who finds who in a game of hide-and-seek or who is at bat in the local softball game, children of divorce have other, more pressing concerns. Is Mom all right? Is Dad going to pick me up tonight?"[21] Wallerstein points out that childhood play is an integral component of development, allowing children to acquire independence and social skills that are important later in life.

Wallerstein also identifies other key ways in which the children in her study suffered over the long term. Ten years after their parents' divorce, one out of three young men and one in ten young women were delinquent, defined by Wallerstein as "[acting] out their anger in a range of illegal activities including assault, burglary, arson, drug dealing, theft, drunk driving, and prostitution."[22] Many of

Divorced couples often continue to fight with as much anger and bitterness as they did when they were married.

the children were coping with addictions to drugs and alcohol, as well as low self-esteem. Barely half were attending or had completed a two- or four-year college, following their poor performance in high school. Wallerstein acknowledges that the problems experienced by the teenagers in her study are not unique to teenagers whose parents have divorced. "Our sample of divorced families, however, shows an exceptionally high number of these children," she emphasizes.[23]

Trouble in school

Wallerstein's ideas seem to have some merit, based on some of the shorter-term studies done on the topic. In particular, the drop in academic performance among children of divorce has been given much attention. "Researchers agree that one should not treat separately the relationship between divorce and academic achievement on the one

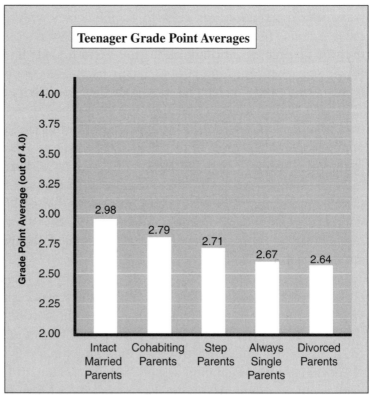

Source: National Longitudinal Survey of Adolescent Health, 1996, NIH.

hand, and the overall effects of divorce on child development," states author William Jeynes.[24]

Experts speculate that children of divorce face various obstacles to pursuing higher education. The first is an increased difficulty in achieving academic success due to the stress of the divorce experience, as Jeynes claims. No matter what the age of the child, if an adjustment disorder is present, it will likely have a negative effect on school performance. Meanwhile, financially, there is often less money available to guarantee that college tuition will be covered. An awareness of this fact could discourage children and teenagers who are having trouble in school (due to their emotional distress) from feeling motivated to overcome their problems.

Promiscuity in adolescent girls

Another possible long-term effect researchers identify involves girls who at first appear to be well adjusted to their parents' divorce. As they enter adolescence, many of these girls exhibit signs that this is not the case. "Entering young adulthood, [these girls] are faced with issues of commitment, love, and sex in an adult context," Wallerstein explains. "Suddenly overcome by fears and anxieties, they begin to make connections between these feelings and their parents' divorce."[25] Having seen their parents' love end, they are less able to trust in their own romantic relationships. Also, since many divorces result in fractured relationships between girls and their fathers—or at the least, less involvement with fathers—self-esteem problems can develop that lead to promiscuity.

"I definitely felt, on some level, that if I had been different somehow my father wouldn't have moved far away, and would have wanted to stay involved in my life," says Ellen. "But he'd been gone for years, and I really believed it didn't bother me, until I became a teenager." During her high school years, Ellen thought more and more about how easily her father had left her life, and she began to fear that no boy would be able to love her. She recalls a desperate need to have a boyfriend—and a willingness to settle for whatever form of intimacy boys would offer her, which was typically sexual. "I wanted them to like me so badly, and I would do whatever I could to make it happen."[26]

Emotionally distant boys

Psychologists find that boys whose parents divorce tend to withdraw emotionally. They share the fears of girls that love will not last and cannot be trusted, but generally respond by keeping a lock on their feelings. While girls tend to search extra hard for a boyfriend, often becoming promiscuous, boys tend to avoid long-term romantic relationships. "Ten years after divorce," Wallerstein notes, "close to one-half of the boys [in the study], who are now between the ages of nineteen and twenty-nine, are unhappy and lonely and have had few, if any, lasting relationships with young women."[27]

Outlook not so bleak

Not all researchers agree that the futures of children of divorce are so bleak. Some critics of this school of thought make the claim that negative effects appear more pronounced when a study is actively searching for them. In *The Good Divorce*, Constance R. Ahrons notes that most studies of divorce prior to hers used only negative questions—for example, "How do you think the divorce harmed your child?"[28]

It is also possible that even being involved in a study on the effects of divorce could affect the interviewees' responses. "Wallerstein looks for evidence that divorce harms kids," writes journalist Katha Pollitt, "and of course she finds it. . . . The very process of participating in a famous on-going study about the effects of divorce encourages them to see their lives through that lens."[29]

Meanwhile, researchers set out to prove the dire predictions wrong through their own studies. In 2002, psychologist E. Mavis Hetherington released results of a major study challenging the ideas of Wallerstein and her supporters. Hetherington's study involved more than 1,400 families and over 2,500 children, including a comparison group of adults and children in intact families. One of the most interesting statistics claimed that 80 percent of the children from divorced families grew up to be "well-adjusted." Furthermore, the worst pain of the divorce appeared to end for the majority of children within a year or two, and three-quarters of the children were functioning well six years later.

In her study, Hetherington acknowledges that divorce is a difficult experience for children. In fact, she finds a significant decrease in well-being among children of divorce in the short term, the first one or two years following the divorce. And over the long term, 20 percent of the children of divorce were still troubled in various ways, compared with only 10 percent of children from intact families. What's

Many teenage girls of divorced parents struggle with self-esteem problems, while teenage boys tend to withdraw emotionally.

more, the problems these children experienced appeared to be more serious than those experienced by the 10 percent of children from the comparison group.

However, Hetherington emphasizes that the vast majority of children of divorced parents did *not* continue to face major effects in the long term and were instead able to heal and move on with their lives. "Divorce is not a form of developmental predestination," Hetherington writes. Just because statistics paint a frightening picture, Hetherington does not believe that the reality has to be so bleak. "Children, like adults, take many different routes out of divorce," she goes on to say. "Some lead to unhappiness, others to a rewarding and fulfilling life."[30]

In fact, as Teyber and others mention regarding short-term effects, Hetherington argues that divorce can bring positive change over time: "Coping with the challenges of divorce and life in a single-parent family seems actually to enhance the ability of some children to deal with future stresses."[31] A group of girls in Hetherington's study convinced her this was the case by displaying exceptional abilities to balance demanding jobs and personal lives and also showing maturity in their approach to relationships.

Ellen, for one, believes there is some validity to this point. Although she did experience, as an adolescent, many of the problems Wallerstein and others warn are likely—most notably a struggle with low self-esteem and a tendency toward promiscuity—she has since defied many of the other expectations for children of divorce. "After graduating from an Ivy League university, I began a career in advertising where I have flourished," she relates. Ellen also got married at age twenty-five to a man with whom she shares what she describes as a very healthy relationship. She credits her many accomplishments at a young age to having had to mature quickly because of her parents' divorce and the resulting challenges of growing up with a single mother. "However," Ellen adds, "I wouldn't say that I'm free of the scars from my childhood. When my husband first proposed to me, I spent a week unable to sleep, feeling an overwhelming sense of panic at the idea of marriage."[32]

Middle ground

While many researchers and psychologists strongly support one or the other of the main schools of thought on the effects of divorce, other experts point out that there is truth to both theories. It is possible, they say, that the negative effects of divorce can indeed be long-lasting for a large number of children—but that these children can still lead generally healthy lives. Studies of individuals whose stories resemble Ellen's lend credence to this idea: Ellen readily acknowledges that her parents' divorce continues to affect her in her adult life, but also describes having succeeded in spite of, and even in part because of, the hardships she experienced at a young age.

Theorists who believe in the existence of this middle ground propose a synthesis of both schools of thought, which they say can easily be found by looking closely at the structure of the two significant studies on the topic—Wallerstein's and Hetherington's. They first note the limited size of Wallerstein's sample and the fact that the participants were all from one socioeconomic class and geographical area. "[Wallerstein's] work is a very valuable exposition of what can happen when divorce goes bad," says Andrew Cherlin, professor of sociology at Johns Hopkins University. "But where I have a problem, is where she claims that her 60 families are representative of all divorces."[33] On the other hand, these theorists criticize the scope of Hetherington's interviews, which were not as in-depth as Wallerstein's. This leaves the possibility that Hetherington's assessment of "well-adjusted" children missed some ongoing problems that were not covered by the questions asked. David Popenoe, director of the National Marriage Project at Rutgers University, explains, "Nobody is saying that [Hetherington's] data is off. But just because you are functioning seemingly well later in life, does that mean you still haven't been hurt and maybe hurt badly in some psychological way by divorce?"[34]

By considering the studies together, with their flaws in mind, proponents of the middle ground claim their theory gains strength. Wallerstein's probing questions uncover the deep emotional levels on which children continue to be affected by their parents' divorce in the long term. The larger and broader sample in Hetherington's study, however, reveals that many more children can move on to happier lives than Wallerstein and her supporters believe. Therein, experts argue, lies the exact middle ground that stories like Ellen's illustrate.

Debate continues over just how disabling parental divorce is for children and what percentage of these children are able to grow up without permanent scars. However, what is clear is that there are numerous potentially significant consequences for children, both short and long term.

4

How Families Make It Through

ALTHOUGH THERE IS no single measure of the effects of divorce on children, no one disagrees that children experience pain and confusion when their parents divorce. With this knowledge in mind, divorcing parents, other family members, therapists, and the legal system can take steps to protect children and mitigate the most damaging effects. These efforts begin at the level of helping children cope emotionally with their parents' divorce. Having identified key problems that most commonly arise, experts can work with parents to devise ways of avoiding them.

Divorced parents

One difficulty experts often encounter when trying to help children through divorce is what Wallerstein calls a parent's "diminished capacity to parent." Parents are themselves healing from the pain of divorce, and their emotions are particularly raw. "It is a fact of life that during the early stages of separation and divorce," Wallerstein says, "children find that their mothers and fathers are much less available as parents; the adults' attention is focused elsewhere. They spend less time with their children, drop routines, let controls fall away, are less sensitive, and have trouble separating their own adult needs from their children's needs."[35]

Some parents are able to work through these problems on their own. Wendy's son, Bill, was a baby when her husband, John, asked for a divorce. Although deeply shocked and upset, Wendy struggled to focus on what was best for Bill. She and John worked hard to establish rules for their joint custody that would allow Bill's life to be as regular and stable as possible, even though being in touch with John was initially difficult for Wendy. "We actually had to learn to communicate better after the divorce, for Bill's sake," says Wendy. "We had to talk about money, and other important topics, without arguing, which we'd never been able to do while we were married."[36]

Some parents seek professional help after divorce. Many struggle to cope with their own emotions as well as those of their children.

Although Wendy and John were successful in their efforts, not all divorced couples can learn to parent after a divorce without some professional help. Parenting programs directed specifically toward providing this service have sprung up around the country. Sometimes parents attend the sessions alone, and sometimes they bring their chil-

dren. Trained therapists encourage parents to keep routines as consistent as possible and to continue to discipline their children with authority. Many of these classes seem to be effective. An Arizona State University study of 218 divorced families showed positive results. Researchers reported a significant reduction in mental health and behavioral problems and in drug and alcohol use—and an improvement in grades—among teenagers who had attended these special skill-building classes with their mothers, or whose mothers had attended alone.

New man or woman of the house

Even when parents are able to communicate about their children without fighting and establish stable, consistent rules and routines, other problems can still interfere with children's ability to adjust to the divorce. One of the most common problems occurs when parents push their children into taking on caregiving roles. For instance, a single mother might rely on her son to reassure her when she worries about their financial situation. Or a single father may look to his daughter to run his household. Gail was seven years old when her father began treating her as his close companion. At twelve, writes Wallerstein, Gail "suffered night terrors, chronic constipation, social isolation, and poor learning. Because her role in life was to stave off her father's psychological problems, she had no permission to be a separate young person with her own identity and feelings."[37]

Some parents turn to their children as confidants, talking to them as if they were adults. "Some mothers in our study relied on their daughters to help with decisions that children could not possibly make, such as selecting sexual partners or changing jobs. They became emotionally and intellectually dependent on a growing girl," reports Wallerstein.[38] Ellen, who grew up with her single mother, recalls that her mother treated her as a partner in the challenges of their lives. At the time, Ellen was happy to be included and trusted in this way. "I felt special," Ellen says, "because my mom told me things that other kids' parents would never have told them, like how serious our financial worries were, or how her dating life was going." As she grew older, however, Ellen began to be uncomfortable with the situation. "First, I started to feel very guilty," she says. "My mom would always tell me about all these horrible things happening to her, and it seemed like it was all because she had to take care of me. Also, when I got to be a teenager, I really didn't want to hear my mom complain that she wasn't happy with her sex life!"[39]

Although many children are flattered at first when their parents treat them like adults, the long-term consequences can be negative. Edward Teyber explains: "Because the natural flow of nurturing from parent to child is reversed, the child's emotional needs are not met. Although [these] children initially enjoy this special relationship with their parent, as adults they come to resent having been used by their parents and deprived of their childhood."[40]

The blame game

Even when parents do their best to maintain consistency in their relationships with their children, some problems are still common. One of the first responses many children have when their parents get a divorce is to assign blame. Most often they blame themselves. The majority of Edward Teyber's young patients say "yes" when asked if they have ever felt they were the cause of their parents' divorce. "Their answers are always the same," says Teyber, "a variation on the theme that they were somehow bad."[41] Children give examples of their own behavior—that they fight too often with siblings or never clean their rooms—as explanations for their parents' divorce.

There are several reasons children tend to believe that they are to blame. First, very young children are egocentric; they still believe everything that happens in the world is directly connected to them. For instance, if the child's mother is crying, the child believes the only possible reason is that he or she did something to upset her.

The child cannot understand that the mother's feelings could be affected by, say, a problem at her job. Even after children have moved past this developmental stage, they still have trouble understanding that something that *does* affect them—in other words, a parent leaving the family—is not linked somehow to their own behaviors.

When children feel responsible for their parents' divorce, their emotional reactions to the situation are intensified. Therefore therapists and other professionals encourage parents to do what they can to eliminate this notion from their children's minds. Teyber recommends that parents explain why they are divorcing as clearly as possible to their children, allow the children to express feelings of self-blame, and then give repeated assurances of *why* they are not responsible for the divorce.

A common problem after divorce involves parents treating their children like adults. This can lead to emotional problems and long-term consequences for the children.

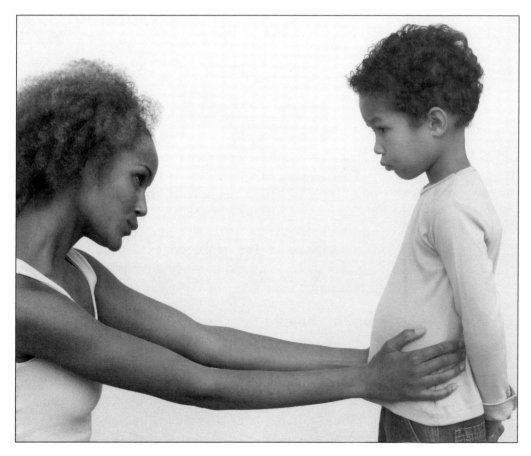

Young children of divorced parents often think they are to blame for the divorce. Older children sometimes find themselves torn between their parents.

For some parents, this is simply not possible. In rare cases, parents are so caught up in their own emotional reactions to the divorce that they themselves make statements that the children are to blame. When necessary, court-appointed social workers will step in to make sure that children are in no way being abused. They will continue to visit the family and evaluate the parents and their children until any perceived problems are resolved.

Out of the middle

Many children tend to lay the blame for the divorce on just one parent, too often because the other parent's accusations lead them to do so. For instance, a hurt and angry mother whose husband requested the divorce might tell the children that their father left them. "In many marital separations," writes Teyber, "the spouse who has been left often feels rejected, hurt, and angry. Too often, that spouse may also feel justified in an effort to enlist the children in blaming the departed spouse for breaking up the family."[42] This can lead to a situation in which children are torn between parents. Experts call this problem a "loyalty conflict," because children feel they are being asked to take sides between their parents.

Loyalty conflicts can occur for a variety of reasons. Sometimes children are pressured to act as spies during their visits to the other parent—to report back clues about the parent's financial situation, for instance, or a new romantic relationship. In rare cases one parent might even make up lies about the other parent to turn the children against him or her. Gayle, who shares joint custody of her two young daughters with her ex-husband, describes her divorce as particularly bitter—a likely explanation for her experience with this type of loyalty conflict. Early in the custody arrangement, Gayle noticed something strange. "[My daughters] would leave my house fine and come back in a week just freaking out," she says. "I eventually found out that my ex-husband was telling the girls things like I was making huge mistakes, and they weren't safe with me."[43]

Experts in the fields of law and psychology, aware of the dangers of loyalty conflicts, have taken steps to prevent them from occurring. Gayle was relieved to learn that the legal system has measures in place to address extreme situations such as hers. The lies her ex-husband was telling their children about her were illegal, and Gayle was able to use this knowledge to convince her ex-husband to stop the behavior.

Less dramatic loyalty conflicts can still cause problems for children, and therapists have worked to convince parents of this. Lana, whose ex-husband has steadily decreased his support payments over the years, understands the importance of not putting her son—the only one of her three children who remains in contact with his father—in the middle. "I never ask him if his dad's telling the truth about not having as much money," she explains. "And I never talk to him about his new stepmother. I know it's important to him to have a relationship with his father, however I feel about him, and I don't want to interfere with that."[44]

Unfortunately, not all divorced parents are able to keep from interfering in their ex-spouse's relationship with the couple's children. Sometimes parents who are especially hurt or angry will use their children as weapons in their fights. Some parents, for example, will seek revenge by threatening to cut off visitation for the other parent. It is the children who are hurt most in this situation, because they are deprived of the connection with their other parent. In recent decades significant efforts have been made to protect children's rights in such cases.

Children's rights

The Children's Rights Council (CRC), established in 1985, is a national nonprofit organization created to support the best interests of children of divorce. Originally formed by a group of parents in Washington, D.C., the CRC now has chapters across the country. They publish a quarterly newsletter, send representatives to testify before Congress on bills that could affect children of divorce, and work with the media to educate the public about the needs of these children. The CRC publicizes a list of rights children are entitled to, including, among others, the right to have "a relaxed, secure relationship with both parents without being placed in a position to manipulate one parent against the other" and "a continuing relationship with both parents and the freedom to receive love from and express love for both."[45] The CRC's mission, made clear in this "Children's Bill of Rights," is to ensure that children maintain the best relationships possible with *both* parents.

The CRC, and most experts, feel strongly that when children are given the "right" to ongoing and rewarding relationships with both parents, many of the potentially harmful effects of divorce are greatly minimized. Wendy has taken this message to heart. Even though her own feelings toward her ex-husband, John, are not always pleasant, she has made a conscious effort to encourage her son, Bill, to feel good about his father.

> [After the divorce] I was always saying to Bill, "you have the best daddy." Or when he would do something funny, I would tell him he was just like his daddy, making him feel that this was a good thing. And if he had good news, or was upset about something, I would say right off "let's call daddy." I never wanted him to feel guilty about wanting to be close to his father, or even sometimes wanting to share things with him that he felt he couldn't share with me.[46]

Financial security

Alongside the emotional needs of children whose parents divorce are the practical needs of survival. Children typically face a drop in their living conditions after a divorce. There are several reasons for this. For one, their parents are supporting two separate households with the income previously used to support one. And mothers, who usually retain primary physical custody, most often earn less money than their ex-husbands. Some children have difficulty adjusting to the changes this different financial status brings, including moving to a smaller home, eating different food, and having fewer possessions than they used to. Parents do their best to make the transition less stressful and easier to understand, but there

Children typically experience a drop in their living conditions following a divorce. This can involve moving to a smaller home, eating different food, and having fewer possessions.

is not much they can do to change the basic fact of having less money.

Courts, however, can ensure that children's basic needs, at least, are met. This happens first during the process of awarding child support benefits. Next, the legal system can make sure that support payments are actually made.

"Deadbeat dads"

Congress decided to address the problem of nonpayment of child support—commonly portrayed as going after "deadbeat dads"—in the 1988 Family Support Act. Effective since January 1, 1994 (delayed to give corporations and individuals appropriate transition time for the new system to take hold), all child support orders must include an automatic wage withholding provision. This means that parents ordered to pay child support may have the allotted amount withheld from their paychecks and sent directly to the other parent. Or, if they are paying the money themselves and are late, the payments will begin to be automatically withheld from their paychecks. Depending on the specific situation, these and other options allow the court to ensure that children are receiving the financial support they need.

Meanwhile, other efforts have also been made to address the problem. Even after the wage withholding provision, some parents would flee their home state and establish themselves in another state in order to evade their child support responsibilities. The Deadbeat Parents Punishment Act, signed into law in 1998, made it a federal felony offense to cross state lines after ceasing to pay required child support payments. Parents who are caught doing so with child-support debts over five thousand dollars could go to prison for up to two years. At the same time, many states instituted programs to help unemployed parents find jobs so they could meet their child support payments.

Despite these efforts, the problem of deadbeat parents still exists, with many dads *and* moms failing to make required child support payments. However, the percentage of payments collected has increased significantly, doubling between the years 1995 and 2000. Experts credit the legal system's increased focus on the issue for the improvements and hope that the trend continues.

Keeping both parents close

Along with financial insecurity, experts identify certain other problems related to divorce that are particularly dangerous for children. For example, children's emotional development and adjustment to life after the divorce can be disrupted and hampered if one parent moves far away or withdraws completely from the children's lives. As Ellen related, many of her problems after her parents' divorce were related to the fact that her father moved to another state when she was still a toddler, essentially ending their relationship. Since the connection to both parents is imperative, families and courts do what they can to avoid this outcome. Many divorce decrees include provisions forbidding either parent to move a certain distance from the other until the children are grown, for instance. Wendy made sure to include such a provision as part of her divorce agreement with her ex-husband, John, because Bill was still a baby when they divorced. Wendy was worried that changes could occur in the years to come that might lead John to move, so she requested a provision in the divorce that prevented either of them from moving more than seventy-five miles from the other.

Depression and abuse

In certain cases, parents are under so much stress from the divorce that they become deeply depressed, even turning to alcohol or drugs to ease their pain. When parents are too depressed to function or are struggling with substance abuse, they are unable to give their children proper care and protection. Social services, working with the family courts, do their best to be alert for this problem and even move children temporarily from their parents' homes when necessary.

In some extreme cases, parents who are suffering from emotional or substance-abuse-related problems take their anger out on their children through verbal or physical abuse. Accusations of such behavior are taken very seriously, and particularly in recent decades courts have made efforts to be vigilant in protecting children from abuse.

Kidnapping

Some parents turn to alcohol or drugs to cope with the stress of divorce. Social services intervene for the good of the children in such cases.

Another important danger children need protection from is the possibility of kidnapping. Some parents decide—for various reasons—that they need to take their child from the other parent. Sometimes the parent keeps the children away out of anger at the ex-spouse or to bargain for a change in custody or support arrangements. Some

parents believe they are acting in the best interests of the children; these parents are concerned that the other parent is harming the children, although the courts have not agreed that the children are in danger. Some parents are desperate for full physical custody or believe they have been unfairly restricted from spending enough time with their children. The only solution, they feel, is to abduct their children.

According to a study released in October 2002 by the U.S. Department of Justice, roughly 203,900 children were kidnapped by a family member in 1999. However, close to half of these children were returned within a week, and the majority were gone no longer than several months. Still, any form of abduction is extremely traumatic for a child. When children are taken from their other parent, from the rest of their family, their school, their friends, and from the security of their normal, daily lives, they face a great deal of turmoil and fear. This trauma only intensifies when the kidnapping does last for a longer period of time. Author Kay Marie Porterfield writes: "Parents who have taken their children often can't work because they will be asked for social security numbers, and often must move frequently in order to avoid detection. Children have to assume different names and may be unable to attend school or even to have friends."[47]

Recognizing the severity of the situation, legislators have acted to discourage parents from resorting to kidnapping their children and to prevent them from succeeding if they try. In 1968, the Uniform Child Custody Jurisdiction Act made it a crime to violate a custody agreement. This law allows parents who take their children to be viewed legally as kidnappers. The Parental Kidnapping Prevention Act, which went into effect in 1980, requires each state to honor other states' custody orders so that parents cannot simply abduct their children, cross state lines, and no longer be held responsible for kidnapping. And in 1997, the Uniform Child Custody Jurisdiction Act was revised to ensure consistency in the policies regulating child kidnapping.

Experts recognize that finding the best way to mitigate the various possible consequences of divorce for children is an ongoing process. Therapists, sociologists, lawyers, and policy makers continue their efforts to help families come through divorce with as few lasting scars as possible. It is widely acknowledged that this task remains complex, and no foolproof methods exist at this point. However, progress has been made, and resources are available for the increasing number of families who face divorce.

5

Society Responds to Divorce

ALTHOUGH DIVORCE INITIALLY affects individual families, sociologists worry about a number of potential consequences for society as a whole, particularly with divorce rates in America remaining in the range of 50 percent. With this statistic in mind, many therapists, researchers, and lawmakers are searching for ways to prevent divorce from happening or at least reduce the number of divorces that occur in the country. Others concentrate on easing the traumatic blow of divorce when it does happen, to prevent the most serious consequences for society. Efforts in all of these directions have been ongoing for many years, with a variety of options pursued.

Divorce affects society

Experts agree that there are clear repercussions for society when divorce rates are high. When the effects on each child, parent, and family are multiplied in high numbers across the country, government resources are strained to cope with problems such as teen pregnancy and delinquency, or single mothers in poverty. "Divorce is never merely an individual lifestyle choice without larger consequences for society," writes Barbara Dafoe Whitehead in *The Divorce Culture.* "Divorce has contributed to welfare dependency and given rise to an entire public bureaucracy devoted to managing and regulating the parental tasks and obligations of raising children. It has imposed a new set of burdens and responsibilities on the schools, contributed to the tide of fatherless juveniles filling the courts and jails, and increased the risks of unwed teen parenthood."[48]

High rates of divorce also influence American culture by affecting individuals' attitudes toward the institutions of marriage and family, encouraging citizens to see these arrangements as flexible and impermanent. Whitehead argues: "A high-divorce society is a society marked by growing division and separation in its social arrangements, a society of single mothers and vanished fathers, of divided households and split parenting, of fractured parent-child bonds and fragmented families, of broken links between marriage and parenthood."[49]

As a result, Whitehead and others who share her view suggest, American society as a whole has become more fractured than in the past. Where members of families used to stay connected and support one another through difficult

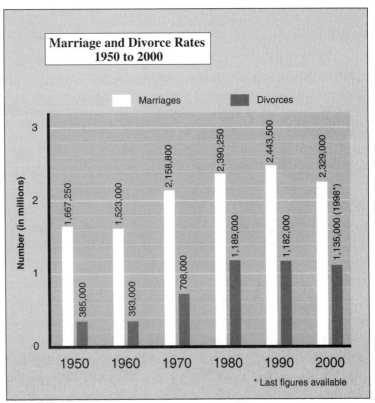

Marriage and Divorce Rates 1950 to 2000

Number (in millions)

Marriages — Divorces

Year	Marriages	Divorces
1950	1,667,250	385,000
1960	1,523,000	393,000
1970	2,158,800	708,000
1980	2,390,250	1,189,000
1990	2,443,500	1,182,000
2000	2,329,000	1,135,000 (1998*)

* Last figures available

Source: U.S. Department of Health and Human Services.

times, now the burden increasingly falls on the government to assist individuals who have lost strong ties to their families. People actually have fewer rather than more freedoms, these experts argue, because the government is forced to play a larger role in families' lives.

"Feminization of poverty"

One of the largest concerns is that divorce has led to a high degree of inequality for women and children, despite arguments that the opposite would occur. Women's efforts to succeed in paid careers and share responsibilities equally with men are hampered by divorce, some say, because divorce typically leaves women bearing both household *and* employment responsibilities alone. Furthermore, women and their children face serious financial difficulty compared with men after a divorce.

Many sociologists refer to this cultural phenomenon as the "feminization of poverty." Over the course of the twentieth century, women increasingly made up a larger percentage of the population of Americans living at or below the poverty line. Researchers point the finger at divorce in particular as a cause for this problem. High rates of divorce have left many single women supporting themselves and their children on significantly lower incomes than married couples have available. "It is hard to think of any recent economic force that has been as brutally efficient as divorce in transforming middle-class haves into have-nots," Whitehead says.[50] And the effect is often passed down from women to their children. Children born of middle-class parents whose mothers fall into or close to poverty following a divorce are themselves less

Divorce typically forces women to both work and care for children. This burden pushes many women into poverty.

likely to achieve the standard of living they seemed headed toward before the divorce.

Few dispute that the high rates of divorce in America have had a negative impact on society and that the problems need to be addressed. But experts have faced continued challenges to the process of understanding how to cope with divorce, beginning with the earliest efforts when divorce rates first began to rise.

Relaxing divorce laws . . . to prevent divorce?

Initially, lawmakers believed the key was to limit divorce to only those marriages that were proven to be diseased. To

Grounds for Divorce by State

State	No Fault-Sole Ground	No Fault-Added to Existing Grounds	Living Separately-Duration
Alabama		✓	2 years
Alaska	✓		2 years
Arizona	✓	✓	
Arkansas		✓	18 months
California	✓		
Colorado	✓		
Connecticut		✓	18 months
Delaware		✓	6 months
District of Columbia	✓		1 year
Florida	✓		
Georgia		✓	
Hawaii	✓		2 years
Idaho		✓	
Illinois		✓	2 years
Indiana			
Iowa	✓		
Kansas			
Kentucky	✓		60 days
Louisiana		✓	6 months
Maine		✓	
Maryland		✓	2 years
Massachusetts		✓	
Michigan	✓		
Minnesota	✓		
Mississippi		✓	
Missouri		✓	1–2 years

accomplish this goal, they kept the list of grounds that allowed an individual to file for divorce as short as possible. Until the early twentieth century, the only grounds most states considered were adultery, desertion, or cruelty. In part coinciding with the modern feminist movement, during the next decades other grounds were added beginning with drunkenness, inability to provide, and insanity, which were recognized as serious conditions that could poison a healthy marriage. However, it eventually became clear that keeping the list short was not stopping couples from divorcing. Instead, couples would often practice something called collusion. In collusion, a couple would come to a private

State	No Fault-Sole Ground	No Fault-Added to Existing Grounds	Living Separately-Duration
Montana	✓		180 days
Nebraska	✓		
Nevada			1 year
New Hampshire		✓	2 years
New Jersey		✓	18 months
New Mexico		✓	
New York		✓	1 year
North Carolina		✓	1 year
North Dakota		✓	
Ohio		✓	1 year
Oklahoma			
Oregon	✓		
Pennsylvania		✓	2 years
Puerto Rico		✓	2 years
Rhode Island		✓	3 years
South Carolina		✓	1 year
South Dakota		✓	
Tennessee		✓	2 years
Texas		✓	3 years
Utah		✓	3 years
Vermont		✓	6 months
Virginia		✓	1 year
Washington	✓		
West Virginia		✓	1 year
Wisconsin	✓		
Wyoming		✓	

Source: American Bar Association

Certain lawmakers have devised ways to make divorce less painful. One example is no-fault divorce, in which couples simply file for divorce by claiming that they have irreconcilable differences.

agreement as to which charge to use in filing for divorce so that they could attain a divorce even though neither spouse had committed one of the necessary faults. This practice was particularly prevalent in New York, which maintained the strictest divorce law, only allowing divorce in the case of adultery. Author J. Herbie Difonzo refers to one observer who joked that New York really had two divorce grounds: "adultery and perjury."[51]

In other states, couples practicing collusion would most commonly choose the vague ground of cruelty, because the term was flexible enough to apply to a range of problems without the spouses having to lie outright. The ground was also increasingly acceptable to the American public due to a change in cultural attitude. Many Americans began to believe that loveless or emotionally abusive marriages were unacceptable. Therefore, they were willing to see cruelty as encompassing a broad range of issues in the marriage. In the 1860s, only one-eighth of all divorce decrees granted in the country were for the ground of cruelty. By 1922 cruelty was the number one ground, and two-thirds of divorce decrees in 1949 were granted for cruelty. Meanwhile, of course, divorce itself was becoming steadily more prevalent.

Lawmakers concerned with the rising divorce rates faced a serious challenge. They had to admit that the traditional notion of strict divorce laws was not proving effective in keeping divorce rates down. As deeply as Americans valued marriage and family, they also valued freedom and individual rights. As one religious leader pointed out, "There are many citizens of highest caliber who profess to be shocked and horrified by the statistical reports of divorce throughout the nation, but yet have upheld and defended individual cases among their personal acquaintances."[52] Many Americans felt strongly that divorce should be a matter of personal choice and freedom. They agreed that divorce reform was necessary, but felt it should allow more rather than less access to divorce.

In the mid-twentieth century, many states across the country began a new practice. In addition to the existing fault grounds, couples could file for divorce after proving that they had lived separately for a certain period of time, ranging from two to ten years (depending on the state), but typically five years in most states. "A nonfault basis, the removal of the need for vicious accusation, and the appeal of an honest divorce procedure: these were the carrots in the living apart statutes," writes Difonzo.[53] Policy makers concerned about high rates of divorce hoped that these "carrots" would lure divorcing couples into a situation that forced them to wait for a prolonged period of time for their divorce. Although the law appeared to be a liberal move, the aim was actually to slow down the rush of divorces and even prevent many from occurring at all. But the waiting period was too much for most couples; the only states with large numbers of divorces based on the living-apart statutes were states with short lists of alternative grounds, such as North Carolina, which did not allow the popular ground of cruelty.

Living-apart statutes were not the only liberalization of divorce law formed with the intention of limiting divorce. The next major effort was the establishment of family courts, which were again an answer that also seemed to satisfy critics of traditional adversarial divorce. With the advent of the family court system, individuals seeking divorce would no longer have to go through the criminal court system. Lawmakers concerned about divorce hoped that family courts—complete with social workers and therapists to help couples and judges evaluate marriages— would allow couples to conclude that their marriage could in fact be salvaged or allow judges to determine this in cases in which a couple's judgment was clouded. Judge Paul W. Alexander, founding judge of the family court in Toledo, Ohio, became known as the pioneer of this new therapeutic approach to divorce. Alexander made the radical claim that the reason previous fault grounds of divorce were not preventing divorce was that they were actually too liberal. Once a specific claim such as adultery or cruelty, whether true or false, had been made and proven, divorce had to be granted under the law—"even if the judge believed that the marriage could be saved," Difonzo explains. "Even if the children would suffer terribly from the dissolution; even if, in fact, the marriage had not broken down, the divorce decree must issue."[54] Alexander and others believed that if divorce were granted only when a marriage could be proven through a thorough investigation to be unsalvageable, then divorce rates would drop.

"Please, Lord . . . let them end no-fault divorce laws. I'll never ask for anything ever again!"

This ideology increasingly took hold among conservative supporters of divorce reform, and liberal-minded advocates also supported a move toward less acrimonious divorce. Finally, in 1970, California made the most dramatic legal move in the many years of divorce reform by becoming the first state to adopt official no-fault divorce.

No-fault divorce

With no-fault divorce, couples could at last file for divorce solely on the grounds that they had irreconcilable differences and the marriage was not working. Neither spouse had to accuse the other of wrongdoing. Couples also did not have to live separately for years, which some critics claimed only stood in the way of possible reconciliation. However, the California law emphasized that a couple could not simply state that they had agreed to divorce, but instead had to explain fully and to the court's satisfaction why their marriage had broken down. This approach made sense to legislators in most states across the country. After California passed the no-fault law, other states followed suit, some—like California—making no-fault the only ground for divorce and others adding the no-fault option to remaining fault grounds.

Reasons for increasing rates

The goals for no-fault divorce were twofold: first, to make the experience less painful and bitter in cases where divorce was inevitable, but second—and most important to many legislators—to find a new way to limit divorce to these inevitable situations. However, many experts feared that the opposite would occur, and divorce rates would climb now that couples had broader access. This theory soon appeared to be correct. By the early 1980s, an average of one in two marriages ended in divorce, and some researchers placed the blame squarely on the increased access to easier and less expensive divorce proceedings. But some experts cautioned that other factors had to be considered as well.

First, sociologists reminded no-fault opponents of the existence of collusion. It was not true, they argued, that prior to no-fault divorce couples whose problems did not fit into the list of fault grounds simply remained married. Instead, such couples would often perjure themselves by a false accusation of a fault, which certainly was not a desirable situation. Also, narrowing the focus to divorce law does not allow for consideration of the influence of other social, political, and economic factors. For instance, following 1970, women entered and succeeded in the workforce in higher numbers than earlier in the century, and no longer considered marriage as a major means of financial support.

Other researchers note the various problems in the attempt to properly assess divorce rates or compare the modern rates with rates from years ago. For instance, Glenda Riley explains that many couples who in the past might have just separated (therefore being left out of census reports on marriage dissolutions) now had to divorce to move on with their professional and romantic lives, because of technological advances in society:

> In an age of Social Security numbers, drivers' licenses, retirement plans, and computerized records, it is increasingly difficult for spouses to go their own ways without engaging attorneys, appearing in court, and filing the necessary papers. Partings that would have once gone unrecorded are now divorce statistics, which expands the divorce incidence and makes it seem considerably higher.[55]

Legislating relationships

Regardless of the reason, divorce rates have remained high. Thus, lawmakers in recent years have returned their attention to finding ways to curb these rates through divorce law.

There is little widespread support for returning to a fault-based system, but bills have been introduced in many states to make attaining a divorce more difficult for couples with children. In Indiana, for example, several bills were proposed in 2003 to accomplish this. One would increase the waiting period for couples who file for divorce if they have children under the age of seventeen. Another bill proposed that parents filing for divorce would have to attend a class on the effects of divorce on their children. The purpose behind these bills and others like them—including ones requiring marital counseling before granting a divorce—is that some couples whose marriages can be saved would halt a divorce process given the chance to think through their decisions more thoroughly.

Some laws attempt to make couples think more seriously before marrying in the first place. Thus, perhaps, couples who do marry will be less likely to divorce. A bill introduced in the West Virginia state senate in 2003 would, among other things, reduce marriage license fees for couples who agree to a minimum number of hours of premarital counseling. In 2000, the governor of Oklahoma began using some of the state's welfare funds to pay for a new program that aimed at cutting divorce rates in the state. The money was spent to hire speakers to hold pro-marriage rallies, classes, and conferences, including classes open to the public on how to maintain strong relationships.

So far there is little evidence that any of these measures, or similar ones enacted earlier in the 1990s, have been effective in significantly reducing divorce rates. However, many of the bills are still being considered, and it will clearly take time before the effects can be accurately judged.

"Better" divorce, not less divorce

Rather than continuing to pursue methods of reducing the divorce rates, many divorce reform advocates argue that America should instead accept that divorce exists and will continue to exist. The focus instead, these individuals claim, should be on making the process as painless as possible for families, which will in turn soften the effects on society.

In 1994, Constance Ahrons published a book titled *The Good Divorce* in an effort to support this goal. On the first page of her introduction, she addresses the apparent contradiction of her title. "Is divorce good?" Ahrons writes. "The answer is a resounding 'no.' Divorce is what it is: a fact of our society; a social institution. Its purpose is to act as a safety valve for bad marriages. . . . But if divorce isn't good, is there such a thing as a good divorce? The answer is a resounding 'yes.'. . . In these good divorces, couples part without destroying the lives of those they love."[56]

Ahrons's book was the first major work on divorce to announce in such a direct manner that this "good" divorce was a possibility. Her book was both an attempt to prove this idea true and a guide for those who hoped to achieve a less painful divorce themselves. The overall argument was that divorce could help a family move from an unhappy place to a much happier one. This being the case, Ahrons and those who agreed with her felt that courts and other professionals in the divorce arena should be working to help more families have good divorces, rather than attempting to keep couples married.

Divorce rituals

Many divorce critics remained outspoken in their objections to this viewpoint, but other Americans agreed with Ahrons. Their approval is reflected in practices such as "divorce rituals." Beginning in the 1990s, divorce rituals are meant to echo the original marriage ceremony and help couples end their marriages in a meaningful, positive way. Ceremonies like these also reflect the emerging notion that divorce is not necessarily a personal failure to be ashamed of, but instead an event to commemorate as a pathway to the next phase of life. Lynn Peters, an artist in New Mexico, founded a business based on the concept—Freedom Rings: Jewelry for the Divorced. Peters holds ceremonies for clients during which they smash their wedding ring with a sledgehammer, and then Peters melts the metal to create a new piece of jewelry for them. "The humor is very healing," Peters says, "and the jewelry becomes a symbol of recovery, confidence, and feeling good about being single."[57]

Various mainstream religious organizations have even begun to hold divorce ceremonies. According to a 2001 article in the *Wall Street Journal*, "Resembling a wedding in reverse, so-called divorce ceremonies can include everything from traditional wedding songs to video tributes to the couple. Also common are ring exchanges (except the spouses take off their rings and return them to each other) and vows ('I promise to respect you as an individual')."[58]

With churches and synagogues holding divorce ceremonies, many American spiritual leaders have joined lawmakers in acknowledging divorce as a fact of life in
America, no longer condemning it as vehemently as they
once did. This widespread acknowledgment has led to the
suggestion by some members of the social service and legal
systems that perhaps the legal terminology of divorce should
be revised. For instance, the words "custody" and "visitation" are perceived by some to send a message that one parent has ownership and the other is simply a visitor to the
child's life. Using more neutral terms instead, many American courts now refer to the "residential" rather than the "custodial" parent and the "access" rather than the "visiting"
parent.

*Parents who take the
necessary steps to
ensure that their
divorce is peaceful can
help their family heal
faster and move on to a
happier life.*

Divorce today and in the future

Some people see these recent changes as a positive step toward a more harmonious, peaceful divorce process with less potential to harm parents and children as they move forward with their lives. Other experts, however, feel that underneath the ceremonies and softer language and attitudes, the basic problems and dangers of divorce remain. Women and children still face financial insecurity, and children still cope with major upheaval and a higher risk for certain developmental and social problems. Men too must deal with financial strain and the emotional distress of separation from their children. And as long as divorce rates are high, these experts warn, society will face the consequences.

It is still difficult to attain exact statistics on divorce, but some experts say rates have actually dipped in recent years and the percentage of marriages that will fail in upcoming decades is closer to forty than fifty. Other experts predict no significant reduction in the number of divorces in the country. No one disagrees, however, that despite everyone's best efforts, divorce remains a very common—and very difficult—process. Efforts will continue to reduce the rates of divorce in the country and, short of that, to address the many problems and questions that accompany divorce.

Notes

Introduction: Divorce—"As American as Apple Pie"

1. Barbara Dafoe Whitehead, *The Divorce Culture*. New York: Alfred A. Knopf, 1996, p. 14.

2. Quoted in Glenda Riley, *Divorce: An American Tradition*. New York: Oxford University Press, 1991, p. 184.

Chapter 1: Child Custody—A Difficult Decision

3. Lena, interview with the author, New York, January 25, 2003.

4. Ellen, interview with the author, New York, January 27, 2003.

5. Quoted in Mary Ann Mason, *The Custody Wars: Why Children Are Losing the Legal Battle and What We Can Do About It*. New York: Basic Books, 1999, p. 16.

6. Richard A. Warshak, *The Custody Revolution: The Father Factor and the Motherhood Mystique*. New York: Poseidon, 1992, p. 133.

7. Dawn Bradley Berry, *The Divorce Sourcebook*. Los Angeles: RGA, 1995, p. 140.

8. Mason, *The Custody Wars*, p. 3.

Chapter 2: Financial Support

9. Esther M. Berger, *Money-Smart Divorce: What Women Need to Know About Money and Divorce*. New York: Simon & Schuster, 1996, p. 136.

10. Berry, *The Divorce Sourcebook*, p. 129.

11. Quoted in Berry, *The Divorce Sourcebook*, pp. 160–61.

12. Mason, *The Custody Wars*, p. 23.

13. Quoted in Mason, *The Custody Wars*, p. 23.

14. Quoted in Mason, *The Custody Wars*, p. 57.

15. Quoted in Berry, *The Divorce Sourcebook*, p. 161.

Chapter 3: Consequences of Divorce for Children

16. Edward Teyber, *Helping Children Cope with Divorce.* San Francisco: Jossey-Bass, 2001, p. 11.

17. Teyber, *Helping Children Cope with Divorce,* p. 12.

18. Beth, interview with the author, New Jersey, April 3, 2003.

19. Teyber, *Helping Children Cope with Divorce,* pp. 21, 91.

20. Amy, interview with the author, New York, April 5, 2003.

21. Judith S. Wallerstein, Julia M. Lewis, and Sandra Blakeslee, *The Unexpected Legacy of Divorce: A 25 Year Landmark Study.* New York: Hyperion, 2000, p. 19.

22. Judith S. Wallerstein and Sandra Blakeslee, *Second Chances: Men, Women and Children a Decade After Divorce.* New York: Ticknor & Fields, 1989, p. 153.

23. Wallerstein and Blakeslee, *Second Chances*, p. 149.

24. William Jeynes, *Divorce, Family Structure, and the Academic Success of Children.* Binghamton, NY: Haworth Press, 2002, p. 20.

25. Wallerstein and Blakeslee, *Second Chances*, p. 61.

26. Ellen, interview.

27. Wallerstein and Blakeslee, *Second Chances*, p. 67.

28. Constance R. Ahrons, *The Good Divorce: Keeping Your Family Together When Your Marriage Falls Apart.* New York: HarperCollins, 1994, p. 17.

29. Katha Pollitt, "Is Divorce Getting a Bum Rap?" *Time*, September 25, 2000.

30. E. Mavis Hetherington and John Kelly, *For Better or For Worse: Divorce Reconsidered.* New York: W.W. Norton, 2002, p. 230.

31. Hetherington and Kelly, *For Better or For Worse*, p. 158.

32. Ellen, interview.

33. Quoted in Mary Duenwald, "2 Portraits of Children of Divorce: Rosy and Dark." *New York Times*, March 26, 2002.

34. Quoted in Duenwald, "2 Portraits of Children of Divorce."

Chapter 4: How Families Make It Through

35. Wallerstein and Blakeslee, *Second Chances*, p. 186.

36. Wendy, interview with the author, New Jersey, March 10, 2003.

37. Wallerstein and Blakeslee, *Second Chances*, p. 203.

38. Wallerstein and Blakeslee, *Second Chances*, p. 98.

39. Ellen, interview.

40. Teyber, *Helping Children Cope with Divorce*, p. 196.

41. Teyber, *Helping Children Cope with Divorce*, p. 68.

42. Teyber, *Helping Children Cope with Divorce*, p. 46.

43. Gayle, interview with the author, New Jersey, March 30, 2003.

44. Lana, interview with the author, New Jersey, March 26, 2003.

45. Children's Rights Council (CRC), http://gocrc.com.

46. Wendy, interview.

47. Kay Marie Porterfield, *Straight Talk About Divorce.* New York: Facts On File, 1999, p. 107.

Chapter 5: Society Responds to Divorce

48. Whitehead, *The Divorce Culture*, p. 189.

49. Whitehead, *The Divorce Culture*, p. 182.

50. Whitehead, *The Divorce Culture*, p. 183.

51. J. Herbie DiFonzo, *Beneath the Fault Line: The Popular and Legal Culture of Divorce in Twentieth-Century America.* Charlottesville: University Press of Virginia, 1997, p. 89.

52. Quoted in DiFonzo, *Beneath the Fault Line*, p. 51.

53. DiFonzo, *Beneath the Fault Line*, p. 77.

54. DiFonzo, *Beneath the Fault Line*, p. 116.

55. Riley, *Divorce*, p. 159.

56. Ahrons, *The Good Divorce*, pp. ix–x.

57. Quoted in Berry, *The Divorce Sourcebook*, p. 201.

58. Nancy Ann Jeffrey, "'You May Now Kiss Your Ex'—Couples Seeking Closure Hold Formal Breakup Services; 'It Was a Really Good Divorce,'" *Wall Street Journal*, May 4, 2001.

Glossary

adjustment disorder: A disorder that children often develop after their parents' divorce, when they have trouble adjusting to the changes in their lives. Symptoms vary in different ages and genders, but include nightmares, bed-wetting, anger, and aggression.

adversarial divorce: A divorce process during which parents are fighting each other rather than working together to find solutions for issues such as child custody and child support.

controversial: Causing people to disagree or object, with strong opinions on different sides.

custodial parent: The parent with whom children reside most of the time.

deadbeat dads: Fathers ordered to pay child support who fail to make their payments.

diminished capacity to parent: A difficulty parents face, following divorce, in being available for their children in every way that they used to be.

egocentric: Believing that one is the center of the universe and that every event that occurs relates to oneself in some way.

feminization of poverty: The idea that, in America, poverty has become more of a problem for women than in the past.

gender politics: Legal and social conflicts stemming from beliefs about gender roles and stereotypes.

gender stereotypes: The traditional ideas about what women and men are good at doing and the roles they are supposed to take on: men as breadwinners and women as homemakers and nurturers.

joint custody (legal): The shared responsibility of both parents to make important decisions about their children.

joint custody (physical): The shared responsibility of both parents to care for their children in their homes.

juvenile delinquency: Illegal or antisocial behavior by minors (under age eighteen), including crimes such as theft or vandalism.

legal custody: The responsibility to make major decisions for children relating primarily to education, religion, and health care.

parental conflict: Tension between parents that leads to frequent arguments.

physical custody: The responsibility of providing a home for the children after their parents divorce.

premarital counseling: Counseling sessions a couple attend with a therapist before they get married.

promiscuity: Being sexually active with many partners.

sole physical custody: The responsibility of one parent to provide the primary home for the children.

spousal support: Payments made by one spouse to the other after a divorce to help the recipient remain financially stable.

visitation: The time that the noncustodial parent spends with his or her children, at either parent's home or at other locations.

Organizations to Contact

Association for Children for Enforcement of Support
2260 Upton
Toledo, Ohio 43606
(800) 738-2237
www.childsupport-aces.org

Nonprofit organization working to improve child support enforcement and public awareness of issues related to divorce and child support.

Children's Rights Council (CRC)
6200 Editors Park Drive, Suite 103
Hyattsville, MD 20782
(301) 559-3120
http://gocrc.com

This nonprofit organization provides support and advocacy for children of divorce. It lists a number of rights to which children are considered entitled, including the right to ongoing relationships with both parents.

National Center for Health Statistics
U.S. Department of Health and Human Services
Division of Data Services
3311 Toledo Road
Hyattsville, MD 20782
(301) 458-4636
www.cdc.gov

The official federal source of statistics on marriage and divorce in the United States publishes both print and online reports, fact sheets, and news releases spanning the past decade.

Suggestions for Further Reading

Books

Heather Lehr Wagner, *Understanding and Coping with Divorce*. Philadelphia: Chelsea House, 2002. Explanation of divorce and advice on dealing with it.

Lenore J. Weitzman, *The Divorce Revolution: The Unexpected Social and Economic Consequences for Women and Children in America*. New York: Free Press, 1985. In-depth discussion of how women and children are endangered by divorce reform.

Websites

Divorce Magazine (www.divorcemag.com). This online companion to *Divorce Magazine* is all about divorce, addressing legal, practical, and emotional concerns for adults and children. There are links to news articles from around the world on numerous topics related to divorce.

Divorce Online (www.divorceonline.com). This website offers resources on many different aspects of divorce, including articles, information, and lists of professionals in different fields related to divorce, such as law and psychology.

Works Consulted

Books

Constance R. Ahrons, *The Good Divorce: Keeping Your Family Together When Your Marriage Falls Apart.* New York: HarperCollins, 1994. Explores the possibility that divorce can bring positive change.

Esther M. Berger, *Money-Smart Divorce: What Women Need to Know About Money and Divorce.* New York: Simon & Schuster, 1996. Clear explanation for women of financial issues involved in divorce.

Dawn Bradley Berry, *The Divorce Sourcebook.* Los Angeles: RGA, 1995. Very detailed description of all practical aspects and dilemmas of divorce.

J. Herbie DiFonzo, *Beneath the Fault Line: The Popular and Legal Culture of Divorce in Twentieth-Century America.* Charlottesville: University Press of Virginia, 1997. Examination of the progression of divorce law in America over the course of the twentieth century.

E. Mavis Hetherington and John Kelly, *For Better or For Worse: Divorce Reconsidered.* New York: W.W. Norton, 2002. Recounts evidence from a study suggesting that the consequences of divorce are not necessarily dire.

William Jeynes, *Divorce, Family Structure, and the Academic Success of Children.* Binghamton, NY: Haworth Press, 2002. Describes a study of the relationship between family life and academic performance in children.

Eleanor E. Maccoby and Robert H. Mnookin, *Dividing the Child: Social and Legal Dilemmas of Custody.* Cambridge, MA: Harvard University Press, 1992.

Explores different aspects of child custody disputes and resolutions.

Mary Ann Mason, *The Custody Wars: Why Children Are Losing the Legal Battle and What We Can Do About It.* New York: Basic Books, 1999. Discusses the theory that children's best interests are not being served by child custody laws.

Kay Marie Porterfield, *Straight Talk About Divorce.* New York: Facts On File, 1999. Provides an overview of possible changes that children and teens might experience when their parents divorce.

Glenda Riley, *Divorce: An American Tradition.* New York: Oxford University Press, 1991. Historical overview of divorce in America.

Edward Teyber, *Helping Children Cope with Divorce.* San Francisco: Jossey-Bass, 2001. Addresses numerous problems that children of different sexes and ages face when their parents divorce.

Judith S. Wallerstein and Sandra Blakeslee, *Second Chances: Men, Women and Children a Decade After Divorce.* New York: Ticknor & Fields, 1989. In-depth interviews, over the course of ten years, with individuals who have experienced divorce.

Judith S. Wallerstein, Julia M. Lewis, and Sandra Blakeslee, *The Unexpected Legacy of Divorce: A 25 Year Landmark Study.* New York: Hyperion, 2000. Follow-up interviews with individuals who have experienced divorce, after twenty-five years.

Richard A. Warshak, *The Custody Revolution: The Father Factor and the Motherhood Mystique.* New York: Poseidon Press, 1992. Argument for fathers' rights in custody battles.

Barbara Dafoe Whitehead, *The Divorce Culture.* New York: Alfred A. Knopf, 1996. Discusses the dangers of American acceptance of divorce and its increasing prevalence.

Periodicals

Mary Duenwald, "2 Portraits of Children of Divorce: Rosy and Dark," *New York Times*, March 26, 2002.

Nancy Ann Jeffrey, "'You May Now Kiss Your Ex'— Couples Seeking Closure Hold Formal Breakup Services; 'It Was a Really Good Divorce,'" *Wall Street Journal*, May 4, 2001.

Katha Pollitt, "Is Divorce Getting a Bum Rap?" *Time*, September 25, 2000.

Yongmin Sun and Yuanzhang Li, "Children's Well-Being During Parents' Marital Disruption Process: A Pooled Time-Series Analysis," *Journal of Marriage and Family*, May 2002.

Websites

Americans for Divorce Reform (www.divorcereform.org). A promarriage advocacy site promoting cultural and legislative efforts to reduce divorce. Offers links to current laws for each state and current divorce statistics.

Child Custody.org (www.childcustody.org). Thorough, well-organized site addressing all aspects of negotiating and defending child custody.

Kids' Turn (http://kidsturn.org). Educational site dedicated to helping children cope with divorce, offering Q & A, artwork, activities, articles, and book recommendations.

Legal Information Institute (www.law.cornell.edu). Sponsored by Cornell University Law School, this site provides comprehensive information on federal and state divorce law with links to sites explaining mediation and custody and offering practical as well as legal advice.

Index

Picture Credits

Cover photo: © Comstock images
AP/Wide World Photos, 22
© Leland Bobbé/CORBIS, 13
© Corel, 9
© Rick Gomez/CORBIS, 45
© Hulton/Archive by Getty Images, 19, 27
Chris Jouan, 41, 46, 68, 70–71
© LWA-Dann Tardif/CORBIS, 32
© Tom & Dee Ann McCarthy/CORBIS, 31
© Mug Shots/CORBIS, 54
© Jose Luis Pelaez, Inc./CORBIS, 42, 72
© Photodisc, 28, 49, 58, 61, 64, 69
© Royalty-Free/CORBIS, 14, 79
© Chuck Savage/CORBIS, 37
© Norbert Schaefer/CORBIS, 17, 57

About the Author

Liesa Abrams has written many books for young readers on a diverse range of topics. She also edits teen fiction and served as editor on the final books in the *Sweet Valley High* series. Liesa lives in the New York metropolitan area with her husband, Sean.